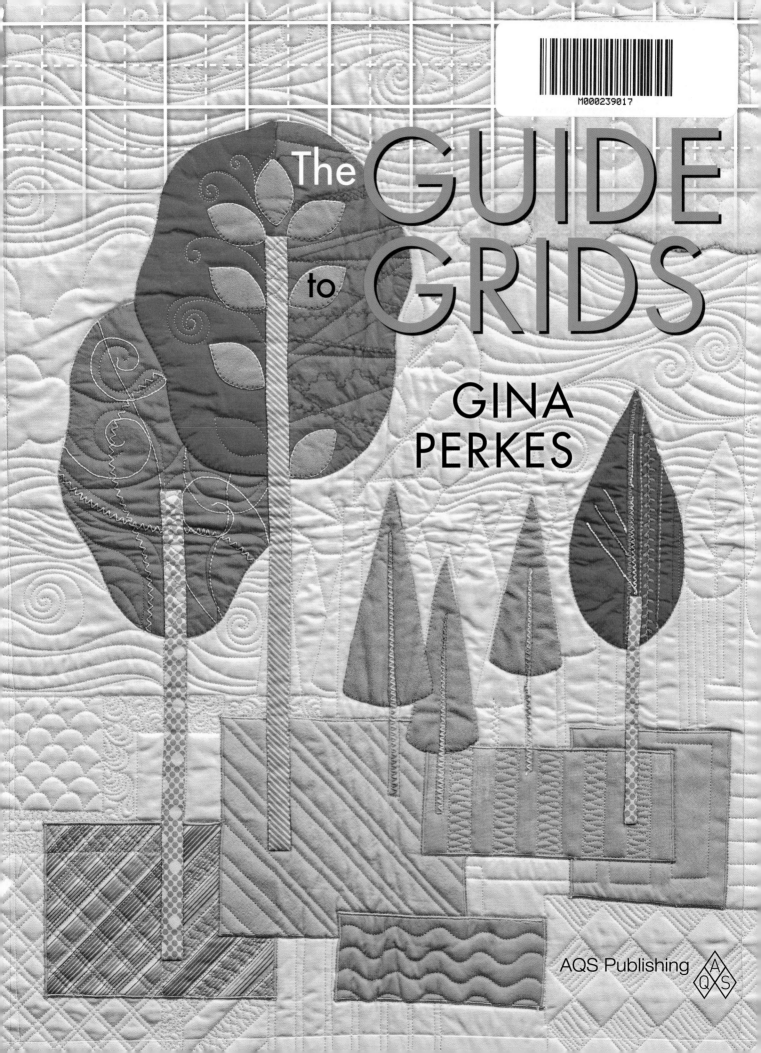

The GUIDE to GRIDS

GINA PERKES

AQS Publishing

The American Quilter's Society is dedicated to quilting excellence. AQS promotes the triumphs of today's quilter, while remaining dedicated to the quilting tradition. We believe in the promotion of this art and craft through AQS Publishing and AQS QuiltWeek®.

CONTENT EDITOR: CAITLIN RIDINGS
PROOF READER: CHRYSTAL ABHALTER
PRODUCTION MANAGER/GRAPHIC DESIGN: SARAH BOZONE
COVER DESIGN: MICHAEL BUCKINGHAM
DIRECTOR OF PUBLICATIONS: KIMBERLY HOLLAND TETREV

Additional copies of this book may be ordered from the American Quilter's Society, PO Box 3290, Paducah, KY 42002-3290, or online at www.ShopAQS.com.

American Quilter's Society
www.AmericanQuilter.com

Library of Congress Cataloging-in-Publication Data

Names: Perkes, Gina, 1974- author.
Title: The guide to grids / by Gina Perkes.
Description: Paducah, KY : American Quilter's Society, 2016.
Identifiers: LCCN 2016043944 (print) | LCCN 2016044158 (ebook) | ISBN 9781683390084 (pbk.) | ISBN 9781683395096 (ebook)
Subjects: LCSH: Machine quilting--Patterns. | Grids (Crisscross patterns)
Classification: LCC TT835 .P352177 2016 (print) | LCC TT835 (ebook) | DDC 746.46--dc23
LC record available at https://lccn.loc.gov/2016043944

Dedication

This book is dedicated to my son, Dalton Perkes. Dalton, you have inspired my creativity since you were two. You showed me how to take time to examine and study nature absorbing every detail. Your natural artistic talent and engineering mind have been a wonderful source of inspiration for me and others. Thank you for always supporting, encouraging, understanding, and loving me. You are an amazing son!

Acknowledgments

I feel so fortunate to work in a creative industry. Having the ability to support myself and my children doing what I love is a gift that I don't take for granted. The quilting world is truly a special place to be. Working with other quilters brings me so much joy and satisfaction. Thank you to those who have taken my classes expressing the desire to grow and learn new techniques.

Thank you to the entire American Quilter's Society staff. You have welcomed me into your family, offering me and my career encouragement and support.

A special thank you to Sarah Bozone. Your talent and patience are both inspiring!

Thank you to my family and support system. I am particularly thankful for my mother, Debbie. Mom, you are so precious to me. I value all that you are. Thank you, sincerely, for being the world's best helper, earning thousands of gold stars daily. You're the absolute best photography assistant, proof reader, encourager, motivator, stitch ripper-outer, and much more! I love you heaps!

Contents

Getting Started

Practice Ergonomics

Throughout this book, we will explore the wonders of using grids in the machine quilting process. Approaches and techniques for both longarm and sit down machine quilting will be thoroughly covered.

We will discuss the process of free-motion, straight line quilting using ruler tools as guides. We will also look at using temporarily marked grids as guides for even spacing when free-motion quilting.

Let's begin discussing some fundamental machine quilting concepts that will be helpful when executing the wonderful grid-based designs that follow. Remember that the more time you spend practicing these concepts and techniques, the faster you will advance and gain confidence in your skills.

Practicing good ergonomics will pave the way for good body positions, allowing you to have the ability to quilt for much longer periods. More quilting time equals quicker progression and completed projects which is the goal for most of us. It may be necessary to remind yourself to pay attention to your body position.

It is normal to tense up when learning new techniques or designs. We can become so focused on executing the design correctly, and we neglect our muscles. Understanding the importance and benefits of good ergonomics will help us to prioritize.

Relax Shoulders

If you prefer to quilt sitting or standing, you need to pay attention to your shoulders. Understanding which movements lead to shoulder tightness is helpful. As you are working, be mindful of your shoulders. When I began suffering from sore muscles and fatigue, I found it helpful to place notes directly onto my machine reminding me to relax my shoulders. They should be relaxed, not strained or tight. Elbow positioning directly affects the muscles in your neck and shoulders. If your elbows are up, and you appear as though you are ready to take flight, your shoulders are likely tense. Always remind yourself to keep your elbows down and close to your body. When your elbows are raised, your neck and shoulder muscles will tighten, which will lead to soreness and fatigue. Keep your elbows close to your body to allow you to quilt for much longer periods.

Adjust Focal Lengths

We all have our individual and unique vision. Different styles of quilting will require different focal lengths. When I am quilting dense and intricate designs that require extreme focus and precision, I need to be up close and personal. In these situations, I narrow my depth of field to focus on very small sections as I work slowly through them. Conversely, when quilting more open designs, such as edge to edge patterns, I prefer to distance myself to attain more depth and a greater overall view. I move through open designs at quicker speeds, so a hyper focus is not as important. Determine where you have the best focus when you are working and make a note of it. It is helpful to have the option to adjust your height based on the design. For example, if you are sitting to quilt, lower your body position when needed as opposed to bending over for a closer view. Many quilters have a habit of adjusting their focal lengths by bending their spines instead of adjusting their chair height. Quilting with a hunched back will quickly lead to soreness and fatigue which will cut your quilting time in half.

I recommend investing in a good, comfortable chair if you sit to quilt. Select a chair that has wheels and a height adjustment option like the office chair shown.

If you use a longarm machine to quilt, use a drafting chair with adjustable heights for custom work if your frame allows.

Another option for changing focal lengths is to invest in magnifying glasses or place a magnifying glass on your sewing machine.

Take Frequent Breaks

It is a good idea to take frequent breaks when quilting on any machine. Changing your body position frequently helps to reduce sore muscles and fatigue. Shifting your mental and visual focus for a few minutes can reduce stress and eye strain which often leads to headaches and/or fatigue.

Free-Motion Quilting

Free-motion quilting, FMQ, is a beautiful thing! It is good for the soul and benefits the mind on many levels. All of the designs and techniques covered in this book are executed free-motion, though some require the use of a ruler as a guide. This means that the feed dogs are disengaged, and you have free movement with the ability to quilt in any direction. The creative world is at your fingertips!

Longarm Free-Motion Quilting

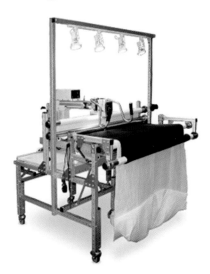

Longarm Quilting Machine

Longarm quilting machines have become increasingly popular among quilters. These machines are set up on a frame system. Quilters move the machine in the direction that they want to stitch. These types of machines do not have feed dogs, so all designs are achieved free-motion.

Achieving Machine Fluidity

Fluidity is one of the keys to successful machine quilting. Whether you are moving the machine or the fabric, you will want to do so with smooth movements. Relaxing is a great way to keep movements smooth. Tense shoulders will likely lead to jerky movements. Many quilters, including myself, find it helpful to have music playing in the background. The right type of music can help you to gain a fluid rhythm while you quilt.

Fluidity with a Longarm Machine

Grip- Pay attention to the way that you grip the handles when guiding a longarm machine. Your knuckles should *NOT* turn white when you hold the handles—this is a death grip. Death grips are bad for your designs and your physical health. Your joints will become sore, and you will become fatigued quickly if you grip the handles too tightly. You may need to remind yourself to loosen the grip. Longarm quilting is hand guided, not hand forced!

Tracks- Always check your track system and wheels for debris. Even tiny lint or thread wads can prevent smooth movements. I clean my tracks and wheels each time I begin a new project, and I am always checking for any build up.

Body Position- Keep your body position in line with the machine. If you are attempting to quilt away from where you are standing, your spine will be bent, and it will be much more difficult to produce fluid motions. Additionally, your muscles will become sore and fatigued. As you progress with your design, simply stop the machine and take a step to the side so that you are realigned with the machine. Always stop the machine with the needle landing in the down position when you reposition yourself. Otherwise, you will add a hiccup to your design when you restart the quilting process.

Sit Down Free-Motion Quilting

When quilting on a Sit Down Machine, avoid heavy hands. Pressing down too hard on the quilt will inhibit easy movement. Instead, focus on using your fingertips to manipulate the quilt. The fingertip movement will be similar to a subtle, easy kneading motion.

When you are executing intricate designs on a domestic machine, keep your fingertips close to the quilting foot. This will provide greater control close to the needle. Open your hands wider for more open design choices.

Intricate design hand stance

Open design hand stance

TIP Keep the edges of larger quilts rolled up or elevated to reduce dragging. This will help you to maintain fluid motions without having to fight and wrestle the weight of the quilt.

Fluidity with a Sit Down Machine

Grip- You will need to get a good grip on the quilt sandwich to move it freely and establish fluidity in your movement. There are many options available on the market for this task. Different quilters swear by different aids. With some practice and experimentation, you will quickly discover which gripping aid is right for you. My preference is very minimalistic. I typically use finger cots or small pieces of shelf liner for Sit Down FMQ. Though there are many great options for my techniques, this works best.

Finger Grippers- Finger cots are placed over the finger, below the knuckle. They are made from rubber or latex which will easily grip fabric. I buy finger cots in bulk. This is my preference because I like my hands to have breathability, and I use my fingertips to manipulate the quilt top.

Gloves- There are many types of gloves that can be used to grip the quilt as you work. Specific machine quilting gloves are available at quilt shops, though you can also use simple latex exam gloves or gardening gloves which are more cost effective. Most quilters prefer gloves that are thin and don't produce much heat.

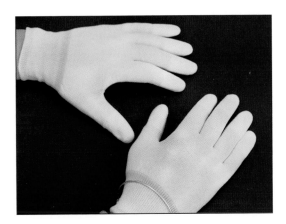

Gripping Sheets- You can use small pieces of gripping sheets, such as shelf liner, to grip the quilt. This is an inexpensive, disposable option that allows you to use your fingertips without having them covered.

Hoops- Some quilters, especially those with joint or gripping issues, prefer to use a hoop to maneuver the quilt. There are a wide variety of hoops available on the market. A good time to learn about quilting hoops is at quilt shows where manufacturers often have them available to try and are happy to demonstrate them.

Comparing Longarm to Sit Down Quilting

There are many different types of machines available in the quilting industry. Many factors affect which is the right type of machine for you: space, cost, skill, etc. It is important to remember that the quilter is not defined by his or her machine. A more advanced, expensive machine does not guarantee success; nor does a basic, inexpensive machine limit it. The only requirement is that you have the willingness to learn and improve. Let's compare two popular and very different types of machines: Longarm and Sit Down.

Longarm Machine

Longarm quilting machines have become increasingly popular among quilters. Many longarm manufacturers now offer sit down versions of their longarm machines, which offer a much greater throat space which contributes to easier maneuverability. Quilters move the machine in the direction that they want to stitch. These types of machines do not have feed dogs, so all designs are achieved free-motion.

Sit Down Machine

Sit down machines are available in many different varieties by most manufacturers. If you are an avid machine quilter, it is helpful to have a large, flat surface to work on. Sit down machines are stationary, which means that you move the quilt in the desired direction to achieve designs.

> *Machine comparison analogy*
>
> Using a longarm machine is like moving a pencil over a stationary piece of paper to draw, whereas using a sit down machine is like moving a piece of paper underneath a stationary pencil to draw.

Stitch Regulation

Many machines offer stitch regulation. This can be very helpful for ruler work, as straight line quilting can be more difficult to develop a rhythm than flowy free-motion designs. Adjust the stitch per inch setting (SPI) based on the scale of the design. For example, choose a larger stitch length (smaller number) for more open, less dense designs. Conversely, choose a smaller stitch length (larger number) for more intricate, dense designs. This takes a bit of getting used to as it is the opposite of the traditional stitch length settings where larger numbers represent longer stitch lengths.

Stitches Per Inch

When using a stitch regulator, you will want to determine the appropriate SPI setting for your design choice. Denser, more intricate designs will be easier to stitch using more stitches per inch or a larger SPI number (14). The stitch length will be smaller which will accommodate tight curves better. When quilting more open designs, it is not necessary to use a small stitch length (11-13 is a good choice for open designs). A smaller SPI number will yield fewer stitches per inch which means that the individual stitches will be longer.

Compare the small, circle design stitched at different SPI settings. Notice how as the SPI are greater, the curve can be stitched tighter. When the stitch length is too long, the circle does not appear circular. The tight curves are not smooth but rather jagged with fewer SPI.

Constant Mode

Stitch regulation is wonderful, but certainly isn't a requirement for good machine quilting. I always encourage my students to become familiar with constant mode quilting. This means that the machine operates at a constant speed. The stitch regulation is up to the quilter. I learned to quilt on a machine that did not offer regulation and found that the machine's sound helped me to find a good rhythm. Many quilters opt out of regulated mode for certain designs such as fillers, for this reason. In addition, when using designs with frequent directional shifts, I prefer constant mode because even the best stitch regulators struggle to keep up with the shifts resulting in larger stitches at the pivot points. When using constant mode, you will need to move the machine or fabric evenly to retain even stitch length. It is helpful to recognize that there is not a default speed. Intricate designs should be stitched very slowly while open designs need more speed. Experiment with different machine speeds, noting the results. You will likely find that the design outcome will vary when stitched at varied speeds. Practice, practice, and practice some more. When using constant mode with a Sit Down Machine, be aware that you can control the speed with your foot pedal. Get those foot and leg muscles warmed up so that you can easily speed up or slow down to accommodate smaller or larger designs maintaining an even stitch length.

Compare the intricate designs stitched in constant mode at varied speeds below:

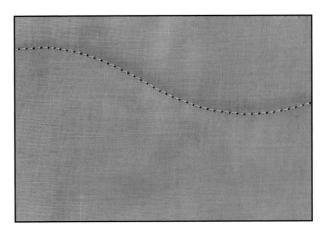

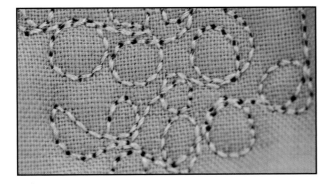

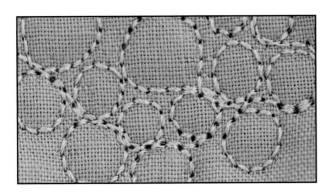

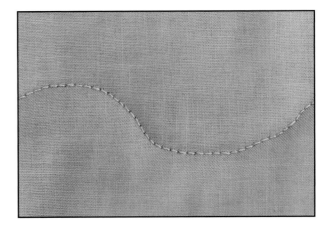

The tiny circles on the top photo are stitched with the machine running very quickly, while those in the second photo are stitched with the machine running slowly. When the machine is running quickly, it is necessary to move the quilt or machine rapidly in order to keep an even, appropriate stitch length. It is extremely difficult to create intricate designs quickly. Therefore, by slowing down the machine's speed, control can be achieved, and the designs can be created with precision and fluidity.

Now compare two open gradual curves stitched in constant mode at varied speeds. The open gradual curve in the top photo has been stitched with the machine running fast. It is smooth. Whereas, the following same design is stitched with the machine running very slowly, and it is much more jagged. It is easier to stitch open gradual curves quickly. Otherwise, we tend to "micromanage" the easy shape.

TIP Play time is very important. When you practice, record your happy speeds based on the design choices. You have found your happy speed when your control and fluidity is good, and your stitch length is even and appropriate for the design.

TIP I cut my sample sandwiches into small, 4" x 6" pieces making notes directly onto the sandwiches as to which speed is my happy speed. I then place the samples into a small photo album that I can refer to often.

Fabric Choices

When selecting a quilting design, fabric choice should be an important determining factor. As you progress and evolve as a machine quilter, you may begin choosing fabrics based on your future quilting plans. A great quilt is one that successfully marries all design elements. Some quilts may focus on the quilting design for the starring role, while in others the quilting may play a supporting role. I find that often the most successful quilts are those in which the quilting designs share the starring role with the patchwork or appliqué designs. When each of the design elements has an important role, visual interest is at its peak. You will want to determine the hierarchy of roles ahead of time so that you may choose fabrics and pattern design accordingly.

Solid Fabrics

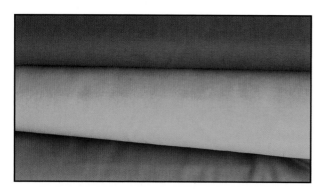

Solid fabrics are very popular and available in virtually any color imaginable from a multitude of different fabric manufacturers. Solid fabrics are a playground for avid machine quilters, as there is not competition for the starring role. Everything points to the quilting design. Regardless of thread color, quilting designs will be highly visible when placed on solid fabrics.

Fabrics that Read as Solids

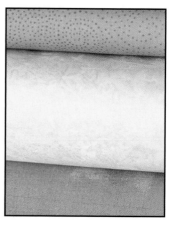

There are many fabrics that fall into this category. These types of fabrics are not completely solid in that they may have a subtle texture or minimal print.

Hand-Dyed and Batik Fabrics

Hand-dyed and batik fabrics fall into this category. They vary in degree of high and low mottling effects. High mottling will create more texture whereas minimal mottling will often appear completely solid. Single color hand-dyed fabrics or batiks will yield the most visibility for the quilting stitches. Quilting designs can be showcased well on multicolored hand-dyed or batik fabrics, though the fabric colors often take over.

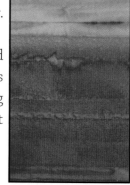

Compare the single-colored and multicolor batik fabrics shown right. The quilting designs will be more evident with the single color fabric.

Single color batik

Multicolor batik

Subtle Prints

Some subtle prints may take on solid-like qualities. Open prints with low color contrast will still allow quilting designs to shine.

The quilting motif shown above plays an important role even though it has been stitched onto a printed fabric. The print is fairly open with low color contrast, so it doesn't detract from the quilting design.

Busy Prints

Busy prints are those that contain high levels of contrast regarding design and/or color. These types of fabrics will typically take over for the starring role. If you want to showcase highly intricate, elaborate quilting designs, this may not be the best outlet. Instead, choose designs that are nondescript in style when using busy prints. This way, the fabric can play the starring role without competition from the quilting designs. When quilting designs compete with fabric designs, the result is visual overstimulation. Quilts should be visually pleasing. When design elements work together, they can be viewed for long periods of time creating positive feelings such as peacefulness, inspiration, or excitement.

Grid Fabrics

Inexpensive grid fabric can be used for practice work.

Some fabrics offer grids in their design. These fabrics are great for practicing and showcasing the techniques and designs in this book. I am always on the hunt for fabrics that contain these wonderful premarked grids as they eliminate the need to mark, saving time. Strategically placing these types of fabrics within the body of your quilt can be highly effective artistically. The creative play between fabric and quilting design is visually exciting! One great quality of grid work quilting is its design versatility. You can use a grid on its own, as in crosshatching designs and variations thereof, for a completely nondescript effect. The nondescript designs are great to use for secondary roles as they do not compete with other designs, such as high contrast fabric prints.

Transferring a Grid to Your Quilt

Individual Line Marking

Individual line marking can be a bit time consuming, though it is a worthwhile time investment. Marking each line individually provides the most control and accuracy for design placement and flexibility for size preferences.

Marking Implements

There are many marking implements available to quilters. Marking onto quilts is always a bit scary as there may be a chance that the lines will remain permanently which would be horrific for a quilter who has invested hundreds of hours. I have had only one negative encounter where the markings remained permanent. For that reason, I only recommend the brands and types of marking implements that I have had 100 percent success with.

Air-Soluble Pen

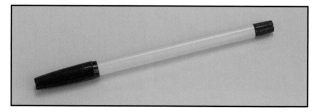

An air-soluble pen is an excellent choice for temporary markings. You will want to mark small sections and quilt them right away as the markings may disappear sooner depending on the climate. Sometimes the markings will last for several days. However, when used in damp or humid environments, the markings may vanish within a couple of hours. To expedite the disappearing time, the lines can be dampened with water. Air-soluble pens have been on the market for many years and provide a safe, temporary option. I have been using this marking implement for nearly twenty years with no issues.

Water-Soluble Pen

A water-soluble pen provides a longer life span. The markings will remain until they are washed away with water. This is a great choice for marking designs that will take time to complete. The blue water-soluble pen is visible on most fabrics with the exception of very dark colors. It is important to familiarize yourself with the removal process. It is necessary to thoroughly soak the quilt to remove the markings. I use a garden sprayer for the job. I lay the quilt on a flat surface, then block the piece back into a square as I remove the markings. Sometimes, the ink will transfer into the batting when wet. Then, when the quilt dries, the lines may reappear onto the quilt. Rewetting the quilt multiple times is sometimes required for the lines to be completely gone. Make certain that you have prewashed fabrics that are prone to bleeding. Otherwise, when you wet the quilt to remove the markings, fabric dye may migrate to neighboring light color fabrics.

> **TIP** Home improvement stores are great places for quilters to visit. This is where you can purchase pressurized sprayers for quick and easy removal of markings. It is important that you use a sprayer that is new or has only been filled with water. Even when thoroughly rinsed, gardening poisons may lurk. I label my sprayer for quilting only and store it safely in my studio out of sight from my nonquilting family members and friends.

> **TIP** If you are unsure if your fabrics will bleed, I recommend washing the quilt in the washing machine, instead of spritzing, to remove the markings. Do not use a low water cycle if possible and include a dye catching sheet in the cycle. This will allow the excess dye to float around in the water then be captured by the dye catcher instead of the quilt. If you only have access to a low water front loading machine, you may want to take a visit to the laundromat. Low water machines may not yield enough water for the excess dyes to travel and be caught by the dye catching sheet.

Ceramic Lead Pencil

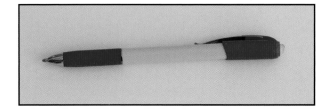

When marking onto dark-colored fabrics, you will need to use a light-colored marking implement. My preference is a ceramic lead mechanical pencil. The ceramic mechanical pencil is preferred by many quilters over marking implements that require sharpening as the lead doesn't dull. A sharper point provides a finer line which improves accuracy and precision when creating intricate designs. The markings tend to fade away upon completion of the quilting process. However, in very high-contrast situations such as black fabric with a white marking implement, the markings may require a bit more coaxing for removal. In these instances, create a 1:1 solution of water and light-colored Dawn® dishwashing liquid. Use a small soft-bristled toothbrush to gently brush the markings away with the soap solution. I use toddler or baby toothbrushes as they offer very soft bristles. A firm-bristled toothbrush may affect the stitch quality or even break the stitches if a delicate thread is used.

Grid Marker Tool

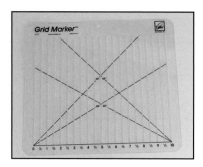

The June Tailor® Grid Marker™ tool is great for quickly and easily marking common grid sizes in increments divisible by ½". It is flexible, transparent, and has precuts.

Chalk Quilt Pounce Pads

Chalk Quilt Pounce Pads by Hancy Creations are used in combination with quilting stencils. This provides a quick method for marking designs onto the quilt. It is important to apply the chalk to the quilt with a flat surface underneath. I typically use a sweeping motion as opposed to a pouncing motion. Secure the stencil firmly before applying the chalk. Otherwise, the sweeping motion may cause the stencil to shift and distort the design. One drawback to using chalk is that it may bounce or rub off as you are quilting. To remedy this, try spraying the chalk with hairspray. This will secure the chalk but will require a visit to the washing machine afterward.

TIP Always avoid applying high levels of heat to any marked lines whether chalk or pen. Heat may trigger chemical reactions which can permanently set the transferred lines.

Marking with Stencils

Stencils have been used in quilting for many years. They provide a quick method of transferring patterns to your fabric.

Cut Plastic Stencils

These types of stencils are very common and available in a wide variety of grid designs. These are the types of stencils that you will need if you plan to use stencil spray as the designs are open. Cut stencils work well for some designs, such as crosshatching and other straight line designs. However, many of the designs in this book utilize intersection reference points. The intersecting lines are not visible using cut stencils, as the plastic remains intact at the bridged intersection points. There will appear to be a break in the line when it is marked onto the fabric, as shown below.

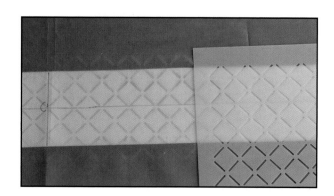

Full Line Stencils

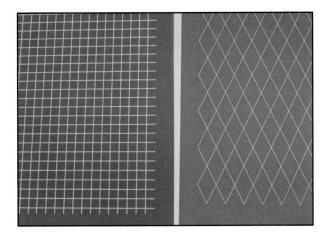

Full Line Stencils from Hancy Creations, Inc., are unique in that they are made using a nylon mesh. There is not a true opening so the designs must be transferred with chalk and cannot be marked with a pencil or any other marking implement. With the stencils not being cut, they don't require a bridge, and the lines transfer fully without broken lines. These types of stencils are excellent when the intersection points are needed.

Take Aim Stencils

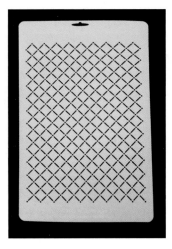

These plastic cut stencils from The Copper Needle (www.thecopperneedle.com) are a wonderful option for many of the designs featured in this book, particularly the free-motion designs. They provide a visible target at the intersection points. Since the plastic is cut, they can be marked with either stencil spray or chalk.

Stencil Spray

Stencil sprays are a quick and easy way to transfer the designs of plastic cut stencils. The benefits of this method are that the spray is quick, easy, and adhere to the fabric well. The drawbacks are that the spray may be aromatic and should be used in a well-ventilated space. It is also not the most cost-effective method. Do not use this method when using the Full Line Stencil brand as the design is not open and the spray will gum up the nylon mesh.

Rulers

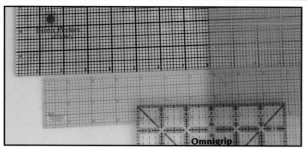

There are so many rulers on the market. It can be difficult to decide which to use.

Rule Features

Size

I work in fairly small spaces when marking grids and find that it is more manageable to use a ruler that is not too big. I most commonly use 2" x 12" or 3" x 15". These sizes are easy to rotate quickly when a lot of marking is taking place. Bulky rulers become cumbersome when marking grids in small spaces with multiple lines and rotations

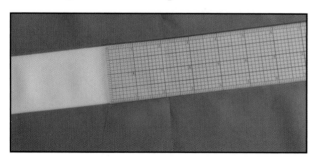

Flexibility

I prefer to use rulers that are flexible. Flexible rulers will bend with the quilt as you mark. When marking a grid onto a quilt that is loaded onto a longarm machine, it is absolutely necessary to use a flexible ruler for the task.

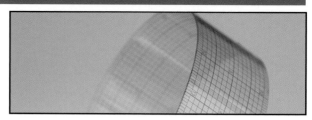

Transparency

You will want to use a ruler that is transparent so that you can see your quilt and initial marks beneath.

Mark Visibility

Consider the color of the ruler lines. Will they be obvious when the ruler is placed over your quilt? If the colors of the lines are too similar to the color of your fabric, it may be difficult to see. You may choose to invest in a variety of rulers with different colored lines. Some rulers provide double-sided markings using two different colors: light and dark.

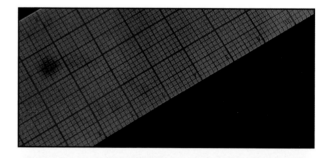

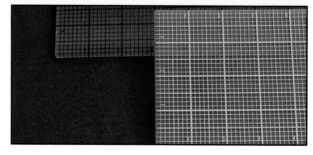

Lines

Line sizes really matter. I like to use rulers that have ⅛" marks. They provide much greater freedom in terms of size variations. It is also helpful to use a ruler which provides additional angles such as 45° and 60°.

Using Rulers with Longarm Machines

Rulers are wonderful tools for longarm quilters, offering exciting design versatility. Longarm machines do not have feed dogs, so the technique is different than traditional feed dog machine quilting. When using a ruler to achieve a straight line, you will need to attach a ruler base to your machine. This provides a stable platform to evenly rest the ruler. It should be understood that a ruler is simply a guide on which to rest the machine's hopping foot.

Using Rulers with Sit Down Machines

Rulers that were designed to be used with longarm machines can actually be used with sit down machines as well. They are typically made using a thick ¼" acrylic sheet. This is a completely different approach to quilting straight lines, as it is done free-motion without the use of feed dogs. Many quilters use a walking foot or dual feed foot to create straight lines in their quilting. When the feed dogs are engaged and the presser foot is in the down position, the sewing machine will only sew from the back toward the front. This means that with each directional change, the entire quilt must be completely rotated so that it is positioned for back to front sewing. Quilting straight lines free-motion completely eliminates this task. With free-motion quilting, the feed dogs are down or disengaged; this allows the quilter to quilt in a multidirectional fashion without having to rotate or reposition the quilt with each directional change. This opens up a whole new level of excitement for straight line quilting with a sit down machine!

Selecting a Foot

It is very important that you select the appropriate foot for ruler work. You must use a thick-edged free-motion quilting foot to prevent the ruler from slipping over it. If you don't have a foot with a thick edge, choose a foot that has a lip edge. If the edge of your foot is too thin, you risk hitting the ruler with the needle. The ruler can slip over the foot allowing the needle to hit the ruler. When this happens, you will likely break the needle and/or the ruler. If you are attempting to quilt with a ruler and a foot that is questionable, do not apply as much pressure to the foot. That way, if the ruler slips, it may not hit the needle. There are specialty ruler feet available. Always test to ensure safety when using rulers.

Foot designed for ruler work

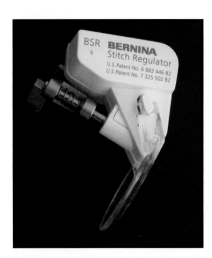

Some free-motion quilting feet have a lipped edge, which work well for a ruler.

Applying Grippers

You will need to apply a gripping implement to the bottom of the ruler. This will be the side that will grip and guide the quilt. There are many different types of fabric gripping tapes and stickers available in the quilting market. You can also use rubber cement found at craft or hardware stores. Rubber cement provides an excellent grip and is easily removable and cost effective.

Guiding the Ruler

The ruler is simply a guide to rest the quilting foot against. Remember to apply pressure over the top in the center of the ruler with a wide hand stance. If the pressure is placed off center, too far away from the edge closest to the foot, you will risk tipping the ruler. When the ruler tips, it may be hit by the needle. A wide hand stance is necessary to keep the ruler stable. Always ensure that your ruler is stabilized both where you plan to begin stitching and where you will end. Once you reach the end: simply stop sewing, with the needle in the down position, adjust the ruler, and continue quilting.

Base

You must attach a base to your machine or drop your machine into a cabinet that will provide a large flat space to quilt. It is very important that your base is at least as big as the ruler that you are using. If you don't use a base or if you use a base that is too small, the ruler will not be stable. Determine the distance from the ruler's edge to the needle following the directions below:

1. Draw a straight line onto your fabric.
2. Place the ruler on the straight line then allow the foot to rest on the edge of the ruler as you quilt.
3. Measure the distance from the marked line to the stitched line.

Once you have determined the distance from the marked line to your ruler's edge, quilt the marked lines as follows:

1. Place the needle down directly on the marked line.
2. Position the ruler against the foot, then line the foot up parallel to the marked line spaced according to the measurement determined.

Maintaining Good Ruler Position

As mentioned in Getting Started, good ergonomics is very important. You will have the ability to quilt for longer periods of time if you are mindful of your shoulder and body position as you quilt. This is particularly true for ruler work. As you hold the ruler with one hand and guide the machine with the other, your shoulders should feel relaxed and comfortable. Remember, you are guiding the machine and offering a straight edge with the ruler. It is not necessary to put a death grip on the machine. Gripping the machine handles too tightly will result in sore muscles and jerky machine movements. The machine can be guided with a two-finger grip for ruler work. This motion should never feel forced—it should be easy. Regardless of side dominance, I recommend holding the ruler with your left hand and guiding the machine with your right. When quilting vertical lines, either back to front or front to back, position the ruler to the left of the hopping foot. When quilting horizontal lines, either left to right or right to left, position the ruler to the front of the hopping foot. Positioning yourself and your ruler this way will offer optimal control. With some diagonal lines that lean to the right, it may be necessary to position the ruler to the back of the hopping foot. Keep in mind that we are quilters not contortionists. Precarious positions will minimize control.

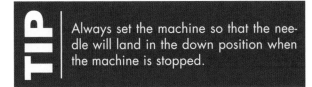
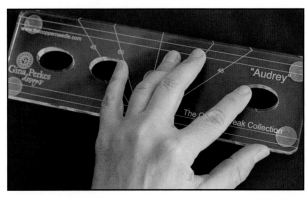

Horizontal Hand Stance

Using Good Hand Stance

Practicing good hand stance will contribute to success in ruler work. Always focus on maintaining a wide hand stance on the ruler with an anchoring finger as shown below. This will provide stability for greater distances. You must support the ruler where you begin your stitching path and where you end. Once you have reached the bottom of the support, simply stop the machine and reposition the ruler. If you attempt to quilt beyond the finger position, the hopping foot will push the ruler. The result will be a crooked line and a seam ripper.

Position the ruler to the left side of the foot when quilting vertical lines either front to back or back to front. When quilting horizontal lines side to side, position the ruler toward the front edge of the foot. These methods will provide the most control and good ergonomics for free-motion straight edge quilting.

To maximize your versatility, practice building straight lines with directional shifts with each new line. For example, vary the direction that you stitch: front to back, then left to right. The design shown below is a great way to master directional shifts. It is an extremely forgiving design that covers a lot of space quickly. It is not necessary to mark the entire design, as its charm is in its inconsistency. However, it is helpful to mark referential horizontal and vertical lines. These marked lines will only be references to maintain the appropriate angles.

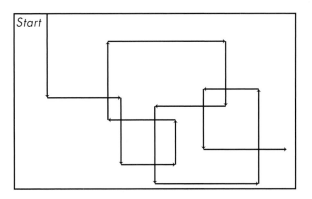

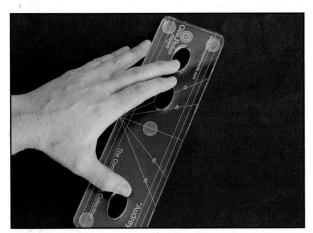

Vertical Hand Stance

Grid Crosshatching Designs

Crosshatching designs have been around for a long time. They are timeless. They have many great qualities that keep them relevant and useful. In my opinion, there are two major factors that make crosshatching designs so amazing: the nondescript design quality and versatility.

Nondescript Design Benefits

Nondescript designs are those that do not take over and/or compete for the starring role. They are typically visually basic without being overwhelming. I believe that most successful quilting designs contain sections of nondescript design work. These spaces serve many purposes: directing attention to other design elements, providing a resting place for the viewer's eye, calming busy prints, etc.

Versatility

Crosshatching designs are almost always successful. They work well when quilted over busy fabrics and solid fabrics. They are quite versatile in that they can easily adapt stylistically. You will see them used successfully in a wide range of quilt styles from modern to traditional. There are many ways to change up crosshatching designs: uneven line placement, uncommon angles, thread color changes, etc.

Placement

Generally, crosshatching lines are most pleasing visually when they begin at the center of the space and build outward. This way, the edges and corners remain consistent.

GINA PERKES

Determine the angle that you will be using. You will need to establish a 90° starting point vertically and horizontally. If placing crosshatched lines in a block, then you can use the block's seam lines as your 90° starting points as shown below. The most common angles used in crosshatching designs are 45° and 60°. Experiment with different angles for exciting and unique results.

If you are crosshatching borders or sashings, use the seam lines connecting the border/sashing to the body of the quilt or blocks. You may also use the edge of the quilt as a 90° reference line.

When marking your grid, do not attempt to mark lines consecutively as distortion may build. Instead,

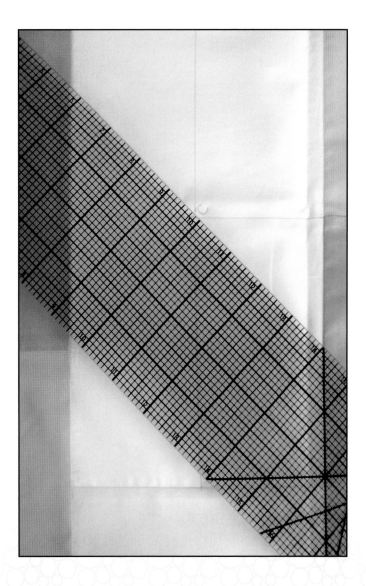

mark a larger open grid, skipping some of the inner lines which can be worked in. This will keep your angles consistent and straight.

In this first step of marking the open grid, you will want to skip some of the smaller inner marks. This serves as an angle foundation. When creating this initial open grid, with each new mark, use the 90° straight edges for reference as shown.

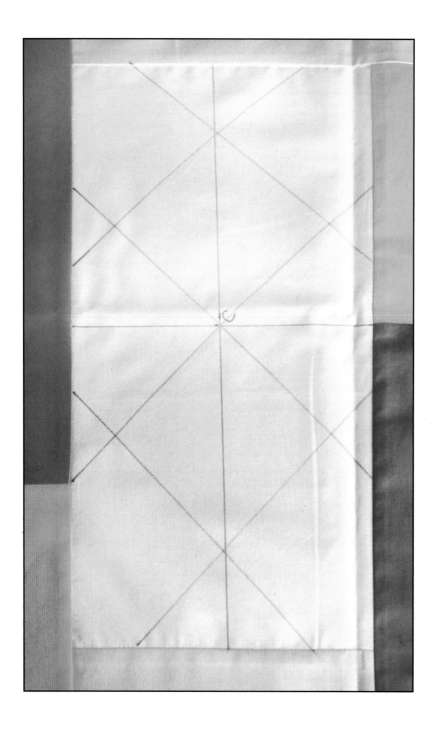

Once you have created a marked foundational grid referencing the 90° sides, it is time to fill in the remaining lines. These remaining lines can be measured off of the initial angled lines as shown.

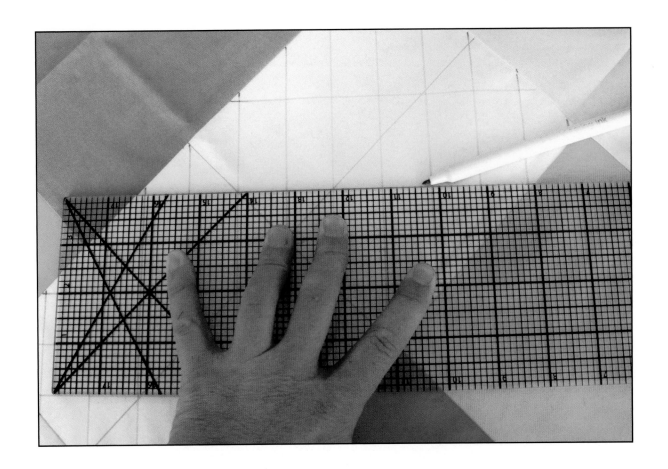

Quilts are very easy to manipulate and distort. This fact is both a blessing and a curse, as often imperfections can be "quilted out." Conversely, a quilt that begins perfectly square can become distorted through the quilting process. Subtle angle inconsistencies are often unrecognizable. However, if inconsistencies build it can become obvious.

Experiment with unique angles varying line spacing for interest. Following are some examples of unique crosshatching variations. It is amazing how a basic design concept can take on so many exciting variations that change the look and style of the initial design completely!

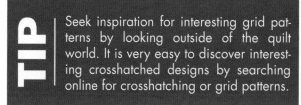

TIP Seek inspiration for interesting grid patterns by looking outside of the quilt world. It is very easy to discover interesting crosshatched designs by searching online for crosshatching or grid patterns.

Stabilization

For success in any custom quilting, particularly crosshatched designs, it is imperative that you use good stabilization techniques. Stabilization is the key to reducing the risk of distortion. This process entails stitching in the ditch (SID) in all of the block and border seams and outlining design elements such as appliqué pieces. You will want to stabilize the entire quilt prior to going back to add intricate quilting elements.

TIP: I use clear nylon monofilament thread to stabilize my quilts. It is truly invisible as it is very fine in weight and lacks the luster that makes polyester monofilament thread visible. In the bobbin, I use a 60 wt. polyester thread that blends with my quilt top, usually a neutral color.

Stabilizing a Quilt on a Longarm Machine

When stabilizing a quilt using a longarm machine, simply begin at the top working through the rows as you advance toward the bottom. When you reach the bottom and the quilt is stabilized, baste the lower edge of the quilt and unpin just the bottom edge of the quilt top. Now you are ready to roll the quilt backwards, plugging in the detail quilting as you work back toward the top.

You must unpin the lower edge of the quilt top before rolling the quilt backwards. Otherwise, the quilting securing the three layers will rip out as they pull apart.

Stabilizing a Quilt with a Sit Down Machine

Once your quilt sandwich has been pin basted, you are ready to begin the stabilization process. In my opinion, if you use adequate pins in the basting process, it doesn't matter where you begin your stitch-in-the-ditch work. Some quilters prefer to work outward from the center. I generally begin at the sides working my way across creating a horizontal/vertical grid. Next, I work inside this grid adding more SID if applicable or outlining appliqué designs if present. As you work through the stabilization process, you can remove the safety pins as the quilting lines will take over the job of the pins.

TIP: Use a large, flat surface for the pin-basting process. Lay the backing fabric down flat (wrong-side up), smooth out the fabric, then tape the fabric's edges to the surface using painter's tape. It is very important to secure the edges of the backing fabric so that puckers or folds do not develop. Layer with the batting, then the quilt top, and begin securing with safety pins or your securing preference.

GINA PERKES

Stitch Path

Stitching the Crosshatch Grid (Backtrack Method)

If your crosshatching grid extends out to the seams of your blocks or borders, you may need to incorporate some backtracking in order to travel to new starting points. *Backtracking* is a term used to describe quilting over previously quilted lines. Avoid stitching lines consecutively. Instead, stabilize the grid by creating an outer box as shown right.

Once this outer grid has been stitched, you can take any path you choose. Often lines will connect, so continue along the path until it ends. If you find yourself at a stopping point, simply travel along the ditch until you reach the next un-quilted line. When backtracking in the ditch, stitch slowly so that you can remain in control and avoid wobbling out of the ditch.

Stitching the Crosshatch Grid (No Backtrack Method with Secondary Travel Designs)

There is so much to love about creating secondary designs that will serve as both creative design elements and spaces to travel from stopping points to new starting points. Travel spaces can be created in many different styles. They can be large or small, fancy or simple. If you want to avoid backtracking altogether, this technique is a great option!

TIP

When learning this technique, begin with filler designs that you are very familiar with and comfortable stitching. Basic fillers such as stippling, loops, or scribble quilting shown below are great choices to learn, as they are simple and don't involve complicated thought processes to execute.

In the first example, we will create a basic frame along the edges of the grid design as shown on page 33.

1. Stabilize the grid as discussed earlier in this chapter.
2. Once the grid is stable, stitch grid lines in any order.
3. When you reach a stopping point where no further lines connect, travel along the travel space using a basic filler design until you reach the next starting point.

After you have worked your way through the grid design, go back in to fill the remaining open spaces in the frame. This can be done once all of the blocks are complete.

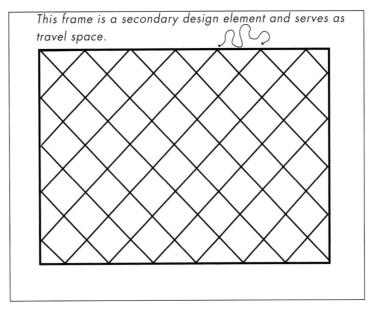

This frame is a secondary design element and serves as travel space.

Appliqué with Crosshatching

In the next example, we will apply this technique to an appliqué block. Crosshatching is a wonderful option to use next to appliqué shapes. As we discussed, crosshatching is nondescript. Appliqué designs are usually eye catching and crave the starring role. Crosshatching designs play an excellent secondary role for these types of blocks/quilts. They direct focus to the appliqué designs instead of competing for attention. The travel spaces will be on the outer edge of both the grid and the appliqué designs. We will use a small echo to draw attention to the appliqué design. Mark the echo for uniformity. You can also vary the style of the frames that you incorporate for added interest.

1. Stabilize the grid as shown.
2. Stitch the grid lines in any order.
3. When you reach stopping points, travel within the travel spaces to reach new starting points.

Design Variation

Radial Crosshatching

Experiment with the shapes and angles of the lines that you are crossing. In the design shown below, lines radiating from a center point are crossed with arced lines.

Curved Crosshatching

There are many great choices for curved rulers that can be used to create beautiful curved crosshatching. Some curved rulers will provide an aggressive curve while others are more gradual or subtle. For the technique that follows, you will need to have vertical and horizontal registration lines on the ruler. Many rulers include these lines. However, if they do not, you can use painter's tape to add them. Always check to ensure that the ruler is large enough to accommodate the space that you are working with. I find curved crosshatching to be the most effective when placed in small sections. Create cross hairs with a marking implement at the center of your block.

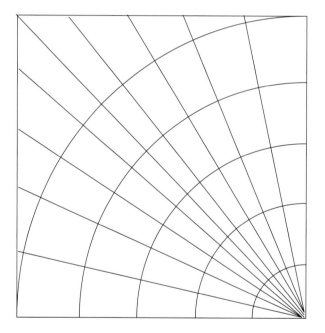

Radial crosshatching is extremely effective in block cornerstones as shown below. In the right setting, this quilting design can add movement, interest, and a secondary design effect.

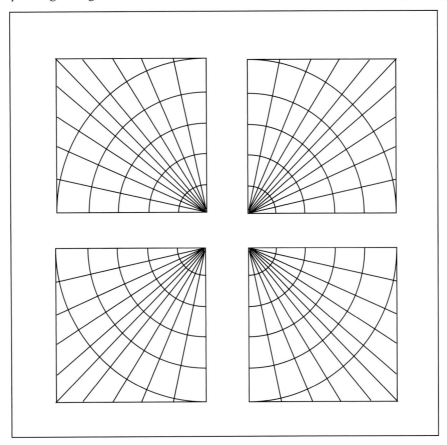

Curvy Free-Motion Crosshatching

For this design, the grid will be temporarily marked and used as a reference for free-motion quilting line placement. This is a great design for adding movement that is structured. It is effective with both large and small sections and works well with both busy prints and solid-colored fabrics. It is beautifully versatile and fun to quilt! This design can be stitched on point or with a straight grid.

This design is created by stitching repeated rows and columns of serpentine or wavy lines that lie parallel to one another. As you build your rows, note the direction that you began in previous lines so that they will remain parallel.

When stitching, strive to develop a fluid rhythm placing emphasis on the intersection points provided by the marked grid. Your eyes should travel across the rows and columns focusing on the next intersection point where you will shift the trough to a peak. Continue to develop this pattern alternating troughs and peaks as shown on page 36.

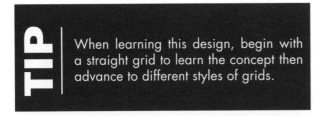

TIP

When learning this design, begin with a straight grid to learn the concept then advance to different styles of grids.

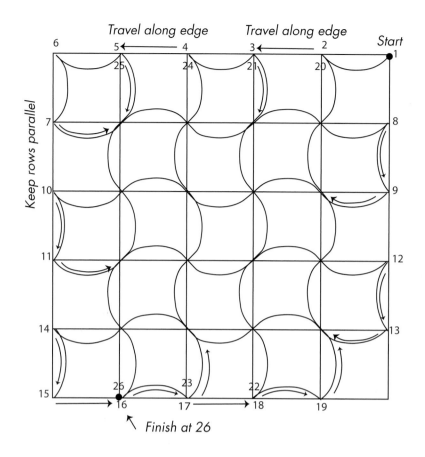

Travel along edge   Travel along edge   *Start*

6   5 ←   4   3 ←   2   1

Keep rows parallel

25   24   21   20

7   8

10   9

11   12

14   13

15   26   23   22
        16   17 →   18   19

↖ *Finish at 26*

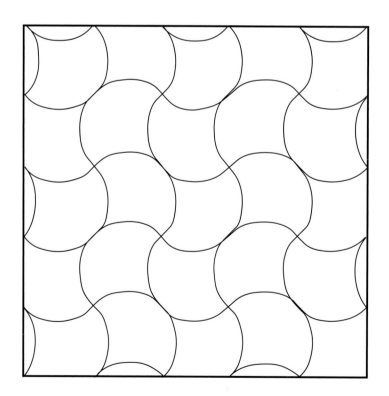

Completed curvy crosshatching design

Secondary Designs

As you are stitching your straight lines to create your crosshatched grid, try plugging in secondary designs at the intersection points as shown below. These designs will likely be small and intricate so remember to slow down your motion to maintain control. The crosshairs provided by the grid will make it easy to place these secondary designs. The results are amazing. You can completely change the look and style based on the plugins as shown in the examples below:

This design takes on a traditional design with the added flower shapes.

This design is more modern with the addition of circles.

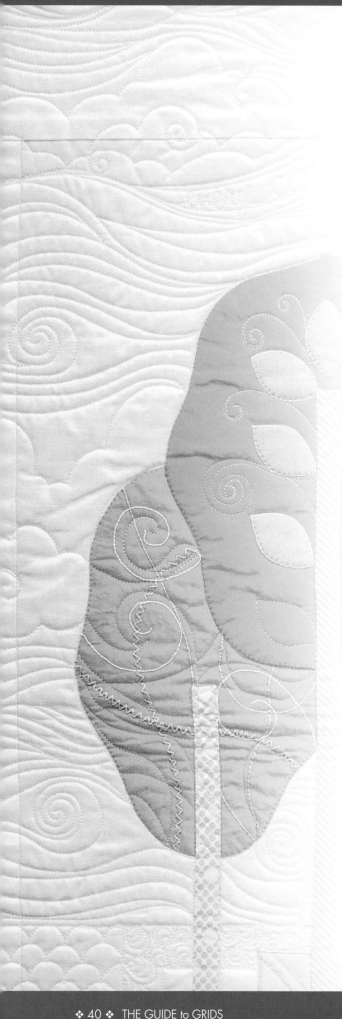

Grids as Guides

Temporarily marked grids provide a wonderful foundation for perfectly spaced designs. Many great designs begin with a grid. We will explore many great designs that utilize temporarily marked grids. Grids provide perfectly spaced sections which greatly simplify the design process. Small, even spaces are much easier to manage than those with no boundaries. With these techniques, not only will you produce fabulous designs, but you will be building some great fundamental concepts that will help you throughout your machine quilting journey.

Fundamentals for Good Grids

Here are some of the fundamental concepts that will be practiced and developed:

Fluidity

Though the designs in this chapter appear very structured, they are mostly quilted with a fluid motion and rhythm. This practice will help you to improve your fluidity.

Target Practice

The intersection points provided by grids serve as targets or points to aim for. Having these reference points will train your eye to look ahead as you quilt. Many quilters struggle with needle fixation. It is always best to look ahead as you quilt so that you can manage the negative space well without becoming locked into corners.

Spatial Concepts

One of the key factors in successful machine quilting is managing negative space. In the designs that follow, we will pay close attention to our stitching paths so that we can be strategic in the direction that we take. By planning our quilting path smartly, we can minimize backtracking and stops/starts.

Clamshell Designs and the On-Point Grid

Basic clamshell designs have been present in quilting for ages. They, like crosshatching, are versatile, elegant, and timeless. By using a grid as a foundation to create these designs, the process is simplified, and the designs can be quilted quickly and easily. Let's explore the basics of this design.

You will need to begin with an even grid that is on point. We will begin with a 45° grid. Identify the zigzag pattern in the rows. Your eyes should move in this zigzag direction as you develop your pattern of repeated scallop shapes.

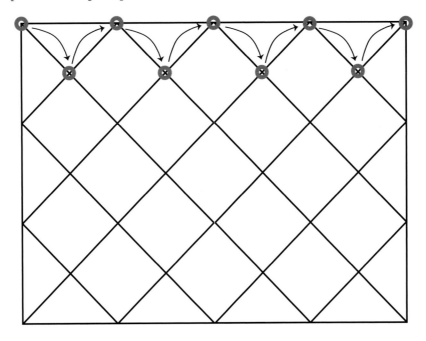

Repeated scallops/clamshells will have peaks and valleys. The peaks and valleys will meet up with the intersection points as shown.

When you have reached the edge of your design, you will need to begin the next row below. As you build the rows, line up valleys with peaks above and vice versa. If your row ends in a peak, travel down the seam or edge line to begin the next row. If your row ends in a valley, travel downward on the angle as shown.

Clamshell Variations

Kissy Lip Clamshell

Double scallops can be stitched to create a unique variation of the clamshell design. I like to think of each doubled scallop as an upper kissy lip. This analogy helps me to keep the design consistent. The stitching technique is the same as the basic clamshell design.

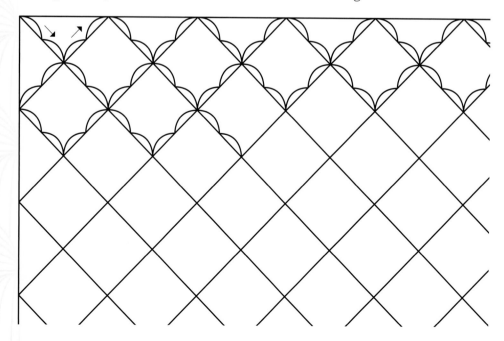

Stylized Clamshell

Stylize your clamshell designs by adding details at the valleys. The style of your design will become transformed by the designs that you incorporate.

As you work through the clamshell design, plug in details to enhance the style of your quilt.

Elaborate detail additions can become overwhelming. Try alternating rows to provide a resting point for the eye.

Consider your stitching path when adding details. Instead
of backtracking, travel back with a new design.

Chevron Designs

You can create chevron patterns using a grid as a starting point. In the example shown below, begin with a straight, even grid. Stitch straight lines from corner to corner in each square segment in a zigzag pattern.

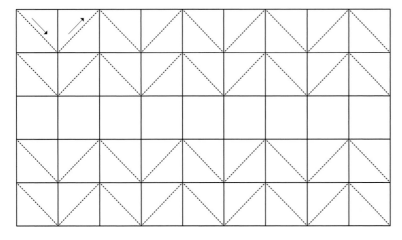

 TIP
It is not necessary to mark the diagonal lines. Simply place your ruler ¼" away from the corner points. If using a larger hopping foot, you may need to place the ruler closer or further away from the points.

Repeat rows by adding parallel rows. For added interest, add a variety of freehand designs in the open spaces.

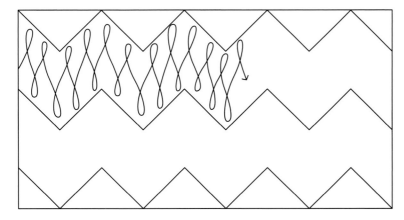

Continuous Curve Designs

Once you understand the sequence of this pattern and practice it a few times, it will become quite simple. Stitching slowly will help you to maintain control with this elaborate design. If you would like the stitches to be less built up in appearance, use a finer weight thread such as 100 wt. silk.

You will first want to lay in the foundational shape which is a repeated subtle S curve. This shape is repeated across one row at a time using a corner to corner zigzag pattern. It is important that the shape maintains the S. The shape is rotated as you advance to the next box but it should not be a mirror image.

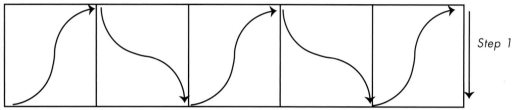

Step 1

Work across the row corner to corner maintaining an accurate S curve.

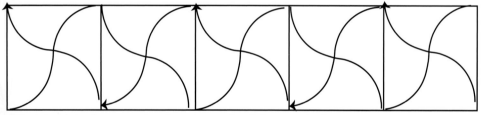

Step 2

Work back in the opposite direction maintaining gradual S curve.

Lay in foundational shapes for any additional rows using the same pattern.

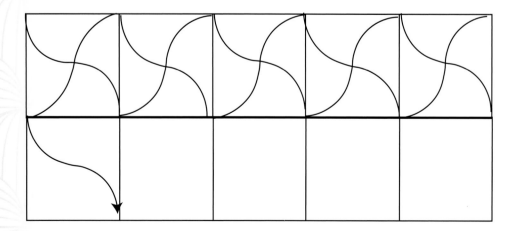

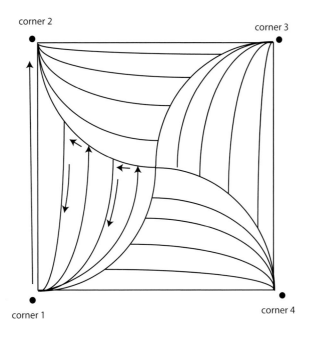

corner 2

corner 3

corner 1

corner 4

Once the foundation is complete, it is time to add the echo detail work. It is important that you work in the order shown so that you can work through a row without having to stop or backtrack. Study the sequence and practice it on paper several times before stitching it.

Beginning at corner 1, echo the inner curve allowing the design to flare out. Travel along the edge of the curve that you meet up with to add the next echo which tapers back to the corner. Repeat this pattern until you end at corner 2. Repeat until you reach corner 3. Repeat until you reach corner 4. Once you have completed this last corner, you should be stopped at corner 1 for the next box.

Continue working through the row in this pattern until it is complete, then work down and across in the opposite direction to finish the grid. The order of the corner echo work is flipped when working the opposite direction as shown:

Once you complete the grid, you will end up with an elaborate, impressive design!

Orange Peel Designs

This design is a wonderful staple design to have in your collection of favorites. It is quite easy to do and has many variations which make it impressive. It can be stitched continuously without stops/starts. I have used this design with the patchwork as my grid and as a border design where I premarked a temporary grid. There are many different applications for this versatile technique. If you are a beginner, use this technique/design to help train your eye to aim for targets rather than fixating on the needle. The intersection points of the grid become your targets. As you hit an intersection point with your needle, move your eye to the next target. Begin in a corner and work in a down, across, back pattern. Make boundary edges obvious so that you know which shape to create. When traveling next to the edge you will simply place scallop shapes. When working through rows, use a serpentine shape so that fluidity will be easier to achieve. At each intersection point, alternate from trough to crest as shown below:

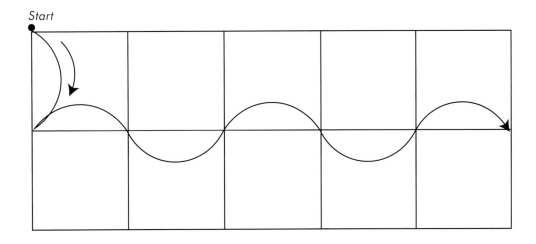

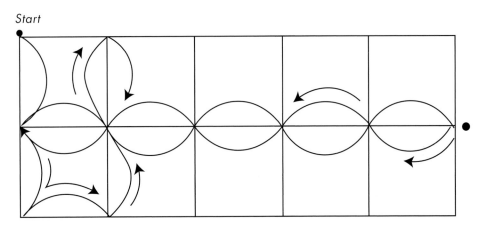

Study the pattern. This design can be used for any size grid without backtracking.

By placing a dip midway in each of the arcs, the design becomes whimsical and even more elaborate. This design is easier to achieve with a larger grid such as 2" or larger.

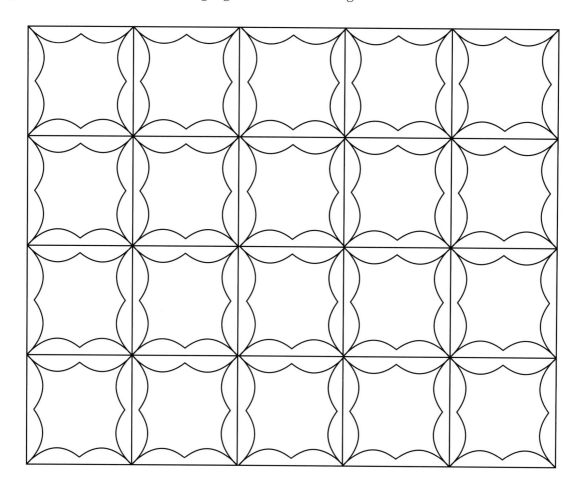

GINA PERKES

Starburst Designs

This starburst design incorporates a secondary design inside the original orange peel design. It is easier to learn this design using a larger grid, 2" or larger. When adding the secondary design, stitch slowly allowing your eye to move from intersection point (target) to the middle of the original arc (target) as shown.

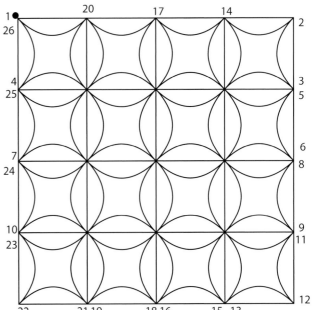

Practice the number sequence to learn the pattern.

Start where you finish the orange peel design.

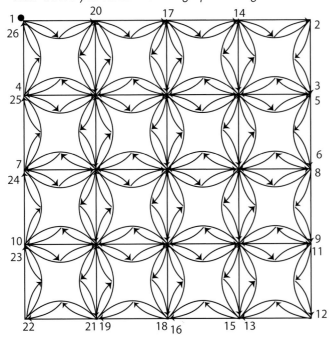

Elaborate starburst design

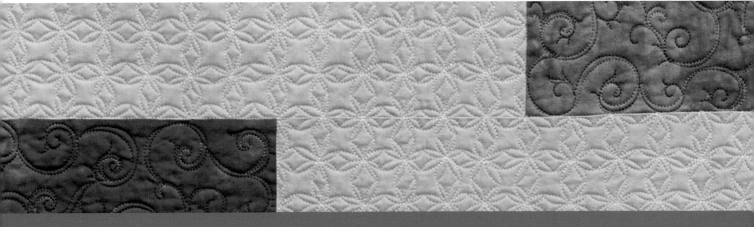

Deb's Doodles

This continuous design takes some practice and thought. Each square receives a double wavy line. It is important that the rows are parallel in terms of the wave's direction. Study the wavy lines below:

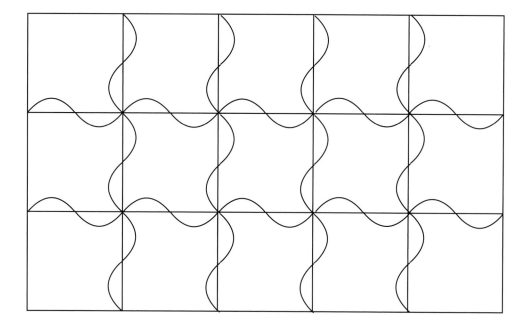

It is helpful to draw a few initial wavy lines so that you have a visual reference as to the direction to begin your row. Pause at each new row to verify that you are beginning your wavy line in the right direction, i.e., the curve is starting to the right or the top.

When you are on the edge, you will simply travel down the edge where the wavy line would be outside of the box as shown below:

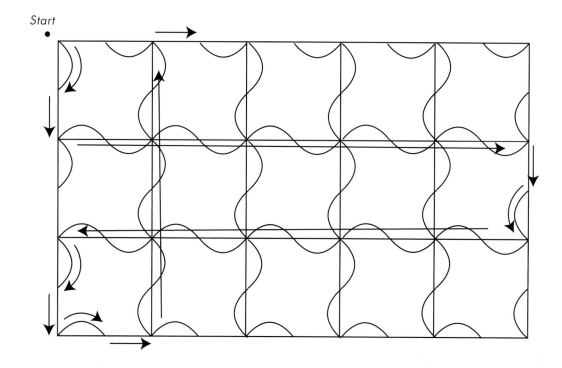

Add simple shapes at intersection points.

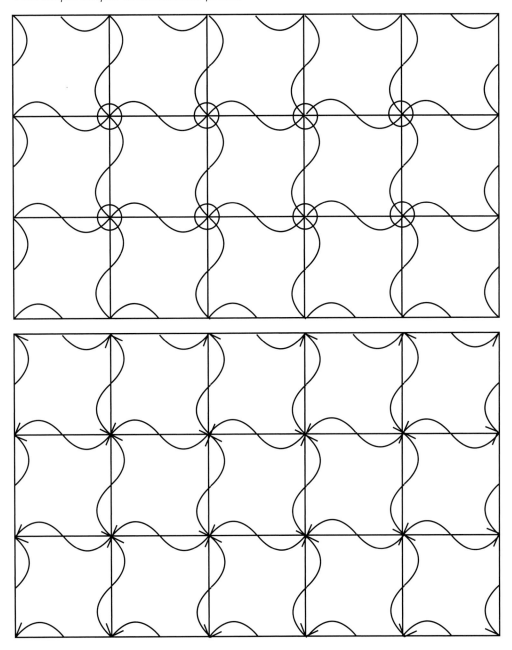

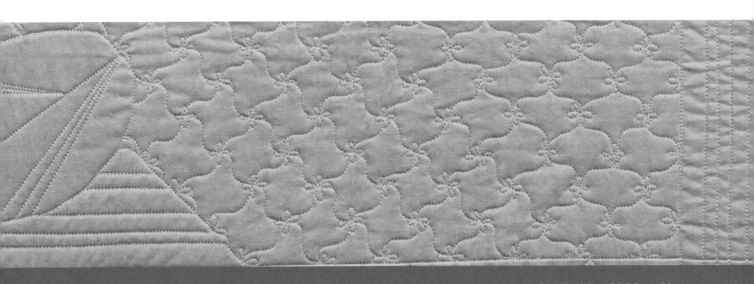

Grid Sashing Designs

Sashing and border sections can be easily managed by using a grid to section and divide them. Determine the size of the grid based on the current sashing or border measurement. One of the benefits of marking the lines individually is that you have more flexibility and control of the size and placement options. Most sashings are fairly narrow so a good starting point for determining the grid size is to divide the narrow edge in half as shown right.

The figures below show a 2" x 12" sashing piece. When divided in half, you have two 1" rows. Since the sashing is an even size, the 1" added columns shown below will divide evenly so that the result is a sashing piece with two horizontal rows and twelve vertical columns.

Some sashings do not provide such evenly divisible measurements, as explained below:

For example, begin with a 2½" x 13" sashing piece.

Divide the narrow edge of the sashing in half: 2½ divided by 2 = 1¼

However, 13 is not evenly divisible by 1¼. Check with your calculator: 13 divided by 1¼ = 10²⁄₅

This indicates that I can fit 10²⁄₅ columns at the 1¼" measurement. Since I want an even number of columns I will round this number down to 10. I now need to determine what size to make the columns, as it will slightly vary from the initial measurement.

Equation: 13 divided by 10 = 1³⁄₁₀
I will make the columns 1³⁄₁₀" apart and will have ten evenly spaced lines.

So the rows are slightly smaller than the columns. Since they only vary by ½", it will not be obvious to the eye.

Often, sashings and/or borders provide a grid in the form of patchwork.

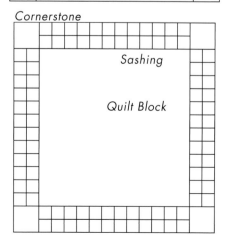

TIP A calculator is a great tool to keep nearby. Most smart phones have a calculator built in. I use my smart phone calculator most days when I'm working at my machine.

Detail of Spring in Prague by Vanessa Fromm of Fabric Confetti

Figure Eights

Figure eight designs work well for all styles of quilts. They are very effective in sashings/borders because they add movement. A great way to learn this design is by using a grid. Establish target sections of each square where you can plug in the simple tear drop shape. When traveling to the opposite square, use a straight line. Avoid curvy connecting lines so that a zigzag design emerges between the tear drop shapes.

Figure Eight Variations

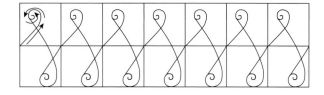

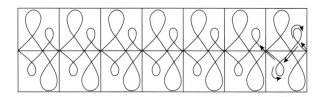

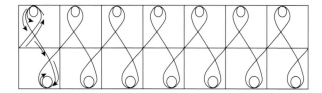

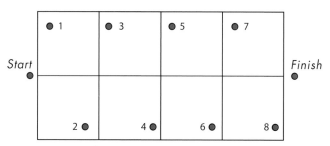

Figure eight target sequence

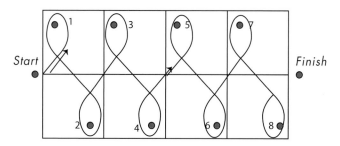

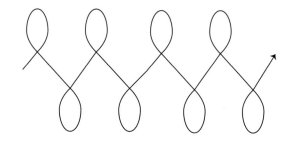

Flying Geese

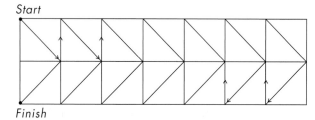

Create design working up one side and back down the other. This way, the design can be created with a continuous line. Your ending point will be the same as your starting point.

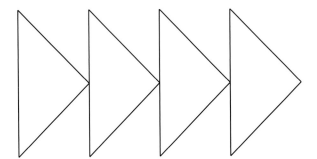

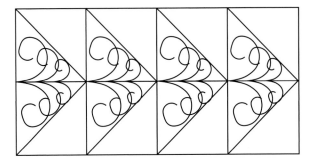

Completed flying geese with grid removed

For added dimension, add details inside or outside the flying geese.

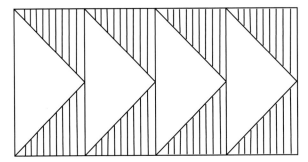

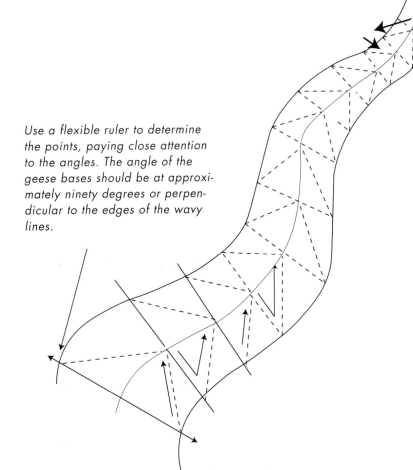

Use a flexible ruler to determine the points, paying close attention to the angles. The angle of the geese bases should be at approximately ninety degrees or perpendicular to the edges of the wavy lines.

Begin with temporarily marking the 3 foundational wavy lines. It adds more interest to taper the ends towards the top and air them at the bottom.

Curvy Variations

Using a similar design concept, you can create amazing movement with the shape of your flying geese. This technique works well along borders or even through the body of the quilt itself. Applying a curvy foundation adds visual interest and directs the eye through the quilt.

Basket Weave

This design looks quite elaborate but is actually quite simple to quilt. It is helpful to create visual references with a temporary marking implement. This will help to keep your wavy lines moving in the right direction. It is easy to fall into rhythm and lose focus. Directional reminders help tremendously. This design looks great along borders and sashings but can also provide an impressive filler.

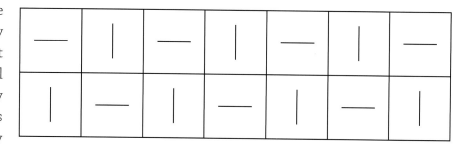

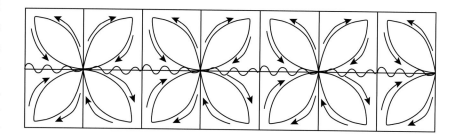

Design Ideas

Study the following designs. They can all be stitched continuously. Use a practice grid to develop the patterns before beginning your quilting. I always have a make-shift dry erase nearby using a grid practice sheet/ plastic page protector/dry erase pen. This helps me to establish a stitching path prior to stitching. Experiment with these designs and create some new ones. The shapes are actually quite simple. The perfect spacing (provided by the grid) makes the designs appear elaborate.

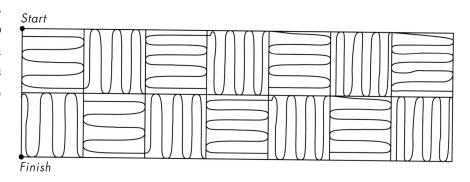

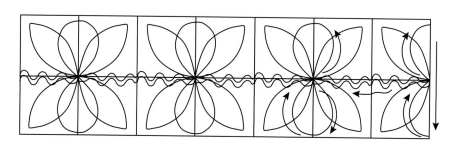

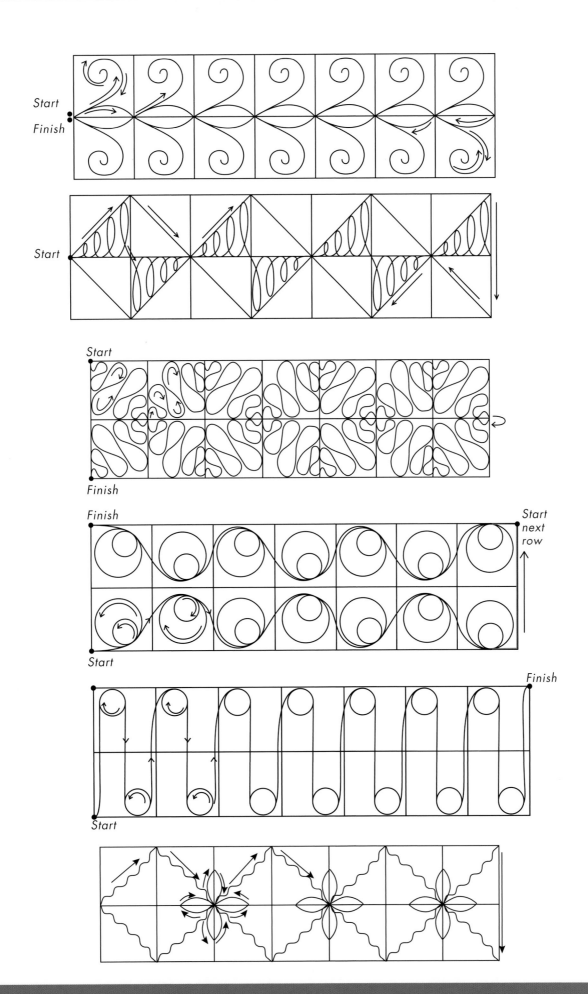

Practice Sheets

Copy these practice sheets to work through the designs in this book. Create a makeshift dry erase board using a plastic sheet protector to place the copies into. Using a dry erase pen, practice the designs and stitch paths.

Horizontal Grid Practice Sheet

Sashing Design Practice Sheet

On-Point Grid Practice Sheet

About the Author

Gina Perkes stays busy beautifying things, sharing her techniques with others, writing books, and promoting the art of quiltmaking. Awarded for her winning quilts, they come to life looking elaborate and intricate, yet the process she favors is simple and easily learned. Creative quilting designs and fills become manageable with grids, resulting in endless possibilities for each quilting adventure.

A lover of all things creative, Gina says she feels completely blessed to have been born an Art-oholic and enjoys all sorts of creative outlets from gardening to mosaic and oil painting. Her favorites are quilting, the culinary arts, and photography, the three passions she relies on to support her Arizona family of three amazing children and one precious little Frenchie named Belle.

Gina is passionate about teaching others and developing patterns and tools for quilts. She has appeared on numerous quilting shows including: *The Quilt Show, Quilt It, iquilt, Linda's Longarm Quilters, Daily Crafts TV, and The Quilting School*. She travels both nationally and internationally to guilds and conferences teaching her techniques on both domestic and longarm machines.

In 2014, Gina was inducted into the Arizona Quilters Hall of Fame.

Enjoy these and more from AQS

Look to AQS Publishing for the latest in quilt topics, surely to satisfy the traditional to modern quilter. Interesting techniques, vivid color, and clear directions make these books your one-stop resource for quilt design and instruction. With its leading Quilt Fiction series, mystery, relationship, and community all merge as stories are pieced together to keep you spellbound.

Whether Quilt-Instruction or Quilt Fiction, pick one up from AQS today.

#12518

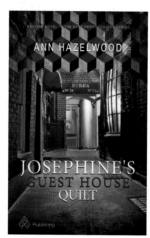

#12061

#12520

#12514

#12516

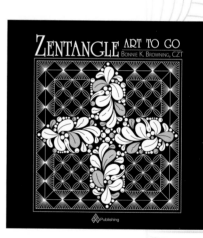

#12512

AQS publications are available nationwide.
Call or visit AQS

www.shopAQS.com
1-800-626-5420